Space Exploration

KINGFISHER
NEW YORK

KINGFISHER
LONDON & NEW YORK

Text and design copyright © Toucan Books Ltd. 2013
Based on an original concept by Toucan Books Ltd.
Illustrations copyright © Simon Basher 2013

Published in the United States by Kingfisher,
175 Fifth Ave., New York, NY 10010
Kingfisher is an imprint of Macmillan Children's Books, London.

Consultant: Carole Stott

Designed and created by Basher www.basherbooks.com
Text written by Dan Green

Dedicated to Otto Wilkinson

Distributed in the U.S. and Canada by Macmillan, 175 Fifth Ave., New York, NY 10010

Library of Congress Cataloging-in-Publication Data has been applied for.

ISBN 978-0-7534-7165-4

Kingfisher books are available for special promotions and premiums.
For details contact: Special Markets Department, Macmillan,
175 Fifth Avenue, New York, NY 10010.

For more information, please visit www.kingfisherbooks.com

Printed in China
9 8 7 6 5
5TR/0817/WKT/UG/128MA

CONTENTS

Introduction
Space Exploration

Top dog in the story of space exploration, I was the first living thing to loop planet Earth, high up above the surface in space. My name was *Kudryavka*—Little Curly—but once in orbit, I became known to the world as *Laika*—The Barker. My journey onboard *Sputnik 2*, in 1957, proved that living things could survive in space, paving the way for human space exploration. Even so, they sent me into orbit without a plan to bring me home—barking mad if you ask me!

Unlike other types of exploration, which claim new territories and riches for nations, space exploration is "for all humankind." The idea is that outside the boundaries of Earth, our differences become unimportant when compared to the might and majesty of the universe. However, humans have only traveled as far as the Moon—one giant leap, maybe, but a baby step in space terms. The environment in space is tough on fragile and squishy human fleshbags, so we use robots for traveling farther. Robotic spacecraft have been sent to all corners of the solar system, and telescopes peer into even farther depths of space. Join them on their voyage of discovery—you won't be "terrier"-fied, I promise!

Laika, the space dog

Chapter 1
Space Aces

Meet the Space Aces, a high-flying bunch of dreamers. The people taking to the air with this set of sky-skimmers have traveled faster than humans have ever gone before. They have also ridden their luck and taken risks that would scare your mother silly! The first humans to go into space were test pilots—they were the only ones crazy enough to sit on top of a missile and say, "Light it!" And yet, Houston, we clearly have a problem! Yes, the Space Aces may "rock"-et, but really they have only just scratched the surface of the Great Unknown: most space flights barely even clear Earth's atmosphere.

Rocket

Orbit

Space Suit

Apollo 11

Moonbuggy

Space Shuttle

International Space Station

Space Tourist

Rocket
■ Space Aces

☀ Gravity-beating engine that lifts things into space
☀ Works by throwing exhaust gases out behind it at high speed
☀ The speed needed to beat gravity is called "escape velocity"

5 . . . 4 . . . 3 . . . 2 . . . 1—I'm a firecracker and life's a blast with me around! I'm used for hoisting and carrying stuff to space. I am a reaction engine, which means I create forward thrust by throwing mass at high speeds out of my rear end.

My propellants (fuels that make me zoom) can be solid or liquid. Since I must lift everything onboard—fuel included— rocket scientists design me with multiple "stages," which are ditched when they burn out. I can even jettison solid-fuel boosters strapped to my sides. These systems allow me to reduce my overall weight during flight. It's a pretty wasteful setup, so some of my newest models use an aircraft to lift them 9 mi. (15km) into the sky. With less distance to cover to reach space and less drag from the atmosphere, I don't need as much fuel. Come on baby, light my fire!

● Escape velocity (Earth): 7 mi. (11km) per second (24,850 mi./40,000km per hour)
● First rocket to reach space: 1957 (R-7, U.S.S.R.)
● Fuel consumption of Saturn V's "F1" engines: 5.2 in. to the gal. (3.5cm to the L)

Rocket

Orbit
▪ Space Aces

☀ The curved path an object makes around a planet, moon, or star
☀ Objects can be human-made (e.g. probe) or natural (e.g. Earth)
☀ An object in orbit around Earth is called a satellite

I am a whirling dervish! I'm the path around, say, a planet, that an object follows when its forward motion balances out the planet's pull of gravity. This is how the Moon circles Earth and Earth goes around the Sun.

If an object traveled any faster, it would shoot off into space; any slower and it would crash down to the ground. No, with me around, the object stays firmly on a course that curves around the planet. The International Space Station and most human-made satellites are in low Earth orbit (LEO), traveling within a few hundred miles of our planet's surface. Polar orbits take satellites over Earth's poles and eventually travel over every point on the surface. Geostationary Earth orbit (GEO) keeps satellites fixed over just one point on the surface, 22,400 mi. (36,000km) overhead.

● First object to orbit Earth: 1957 (*Sputnik 1*, U.S.S.R.)
● First human to orbit Earth: 1961 (Yuri Gagarin, U.S.S.R.)
● Official start of space: 60 mi. (100km) (known as the Kármán line)

Orbit

Space Suit
■ Space Aces

✳ Tough protection for astronauts outside their spacecraft
✳ Features a bubble helmet with a gold, radiation-blocking visor
✳ Color-coded legs help identify astronauts in space

Hi! I'm an Extravehicular Mobility Unit (EMU for short), and I do my utmost to protect puny humans from the harsh environment of space. Don't step outside without me!

My modular design uses clip-together parts to make a pressurized suit that stops blood and body fluids from boiling in the near-vacuum of space. As many as 14 layers offer comfort and safety. The outermost shell is made from supertough Kevlar, which provides protection from flying micrometeorites. Five thin aluminum sheets block most radiation. My primary life-support system provides oxygen to breathe, and my gloves have a battery-powered heater in each finger. Crazy undergarments with stitched-in, liquid-cooled pipework deal with the heat astronauts generate. I like to keep 'em cool, calm, and collected.

● Number of parts in a typical space suit: about 18,000
● Length of pipes in undergarments: 300 ft. (91.5m)
● Typical weight: 276 lb. (125kg)

Space Suit

Apollo 11

■ Space Aces

☀ Three-stage lunar mission, launched by *Saturn V* rocket
☀ The lunar module landed on the Moon on July 20, 1969
☀ This tin can was nicknamed "Eagle"

I was the all-American hero who was the first to take astronauts (Neil Armstrong, "Buzz" Aldrin, and Michael Collins) to the Moon. Armstrong took the "Eagle" down to the surface with Aldrin, while Collins stayed in orbit in my command module. Armstrong stepped out onto the Moon with the immortal words, "One small step for man, one giant leap for mankind."

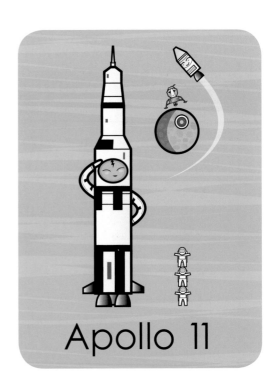

Apollo 11

● Height of *Saturn V* rocket: 364 ft. (111m)
● Mass of *Saturn V*: 3,200 tons (2,900,000kg) (650 elephants)
● Time "Eagle" spent on the surface of the Moon: 21.5 hours

Moonbuggy
Space Aces ■

- ✴ The last word in electric-powered off-road vehicles
- ✴ This speedy cart was used on Apollo missions 15, 16, and 17
- ✴ Its official name is Lunar Roving Vehicle (LRV)

Moonbuggy

What's better than walking on the Moon? Why, surely, it's *driving* on the Moon! With my light, aluminum frame, mesh wheels, and nylon-strapping bucket seats, I allowed astronauts to range much farther than they had on previous landings. I was transported to the Moon on the last three Apollo missions, strapped to the outside of the lunar module, just like dirt bikes on an RV!

- ● Longest single trip: 12.5 mi. (20.1km)
- ● Lunar land-speed record: 11 mph (18km/h) (Eugene Cernan)
- ● Power: 2 x 36-V batteries

Space Shuttle
Space Aces

* The first reusable, winged "space plane"
* The five shuttles included *Discovery*, *Endeavour*, and *Atlantis*
* *Challenger* and *Columbia* were lost in fatal accidents

I'm the Granddaddy—the largest spacecraft ever to travel to space. I'm retired now, but for a good 30 years I was the workhorse of the U.S. space program. I lifted and carried people and equipment into low Earth orbit (LEO).

I had space for two satellites or a space lab in my payload bay. I took the Hubble Space Telescope into orbit and transported many International Space Station modules. Made from clip-together parts, I had a space plane called the Orbiter with a big, external fuel tank (ET) slung beneath and two solid rocket boosters (SRBs) clipped to that. Firing both SRBs and the main engines, I took to the skies. After two minutes, the burned-out SRBs were jettisoned; six minutes later, the ET was released. Gliding back to Earth, my Orbiter would touch down at 220 mph (350km/h). Happy days!

● First Space Shuttle flight: April 12, 1981 (*Columbia*)
● Last Space Shuttle lands after final flight: July 21, 2011 (*Atlantis*)
● Number of Space Shuttle launches: 135

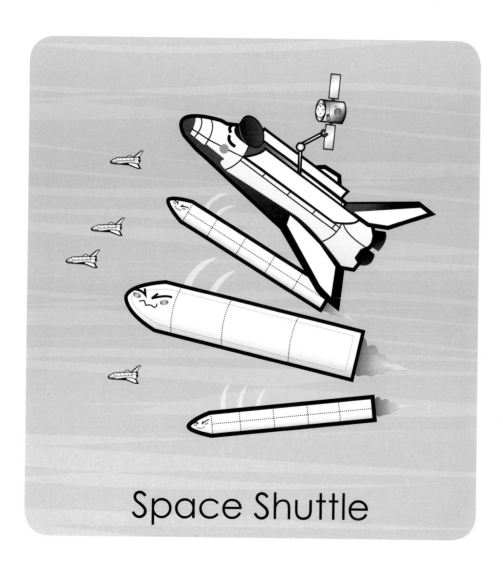

Space Shuttle

International Space Station

Space Aces

* AKA the ISS—an orbiting space laboratory in low Earth orbit
* Built from 1998 to 2011, using contributions from 16 nations
* The third-brightest object in the sky after the Sun and Moon

Cruisin' at 240 mi. (390km) above Earth, I'm like a diamond in the sky. The most expensive science project *ever*, I'm a bustling space hub, built piece by piece over more than ten years.

I'm built on a long truss bolted together in space. Off this structure hang double-sided, Sun-tracking solar arrays that provide power, temperature-regulating radiators, living quarters, and laboratories. Life is buzzing with plenty of experiments to fill a ten-hour working day. Astronauts stay for up to six months, breathing stale air and drinking (ahem) "recycled" water, eating ready-made dinners, and sleeping tethered to a metal wall. However, they do get to see 15 sunrises and sunsets every day. Beat that, Earth dwellers!

- First component launched: 1998 (Zarya, Russian Federal Space Agency)
- Orbital speed: 17,210 mph (27,700km/h)
- Living space: 13,702 cu. ft. (388 cu. m)

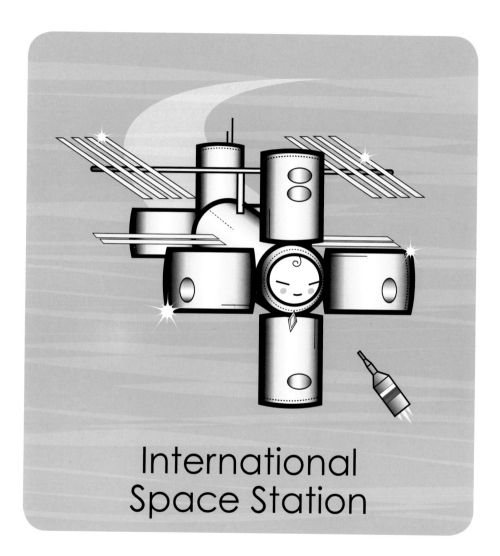

International Space Station

Space Tourist
■ Space Aces

* Megabucks business dude who tags along on space missions
* Known as a "participant," not an "astronaut"
* Is expected to help out with tasks onboard the spacecraft

I'm off on a space vacation—a "spa-cation," if you like! The flight is awesome, and the weather is interesting (–148°F/ –100°C in the shade, 248°F/120°C in the Sun). There's a slight chance of some deadly radiation, but, hey, I get to see my home planet hanging tiny and fragile in the vastness of space!

Soyuz—operated by the Russian Federal Space Agency—is my taxi to the ISS. Traveling to the space station is the big one, and the trip that costs the most, but there are other options. How about a ticket for an orbital day trip (flying 60 mi./ 100km above Earth for at least one loop)? Or a suborbital day trip (flying above 60 mi./100km into space, but returning before a complete orbit of Earth is made)? There is also talk of cruises to the Moon in the future and maybe even a space hotel. Room service might be expensive, though!

● First fee-paying tourist: Dennis Tito, April 28, 2001 ($20 million)
● First commercial spacecraft to dock with ISS: May 25, 2012 (*Dragon* capsule)
● Space endurance record: 437.7 days (Valeri Polyakov, on Russia's Mir space station)

Space Tourist

Chapter 2
Sunshine Superstars

These Sun-skimming superheroes are the spacecraft tasked with exploring our star and the rocky "terrestrial" planets orbiting close to it—Mercury, Venus, Earth, and Mars. These guys withstand SIZZLING temperatures—hot enough to make exposed metal reach 500°F (260°C)—and a barrage of circuit-frying radiation from the Sun. Many of them turn their instruments back on Earth, to study our home planet in ever-greater detail. Mighty Mars is a popular destination, but so many have been lost on these missions that astro-scientists joke about a "Great Galactic Ghoul" who feeds on Mars probes. Shudder!

STEREO

MESSENGER

Venus Express

Sputnik 1

Satellite

Mars
Reconnaissance
Orbiter

Curiosity

Dawn

STEREO
Sunshine Superstars

- A pair of Sun seekers built and operated by NASA
- Orbit the Sun in front of and behind planet Earth
- Perform the task of space-weather forecasting

Apply the SPF 15, stick on the shades, and step into the glare. We twin satellites peer directly into the great ball of fire in the sky. Yes, we keep an eye on the Sun.

We raise the alarm about huge, explosive eruptions that blast massive bursts of material out of the Sun and into space. We're talking billions of tons of solar material that, should it reach Earth, would knock out communications satellites and power grids. The thing is, the Sun spins so slowly that if trouble brews on the far side, Earth-based observatories can't spot it in time. Enter *STEREO A* and *STEREO B*! When launched, *A* sped ahead of planet Earth and *B* fell behind so that, four years later, we were directly opposite each other on either side of the Sun. With 180° separation, we can see the whole Sun at a glance. Wow!

- Launch date: October 25, 2006
- Coronal Mass Ejection (CME): name given to the Sun's explosive eruptions
- Name stands for **S**olar **TE**rrestrial **RE**lations **O**bservatory

STEREO

MESSENGER
Sunshine Superstars

✺ Hot-footed space probe from NASA's Discovery Program
✺ The only spacecraft ever to orbit planet Mercury
✺ The first spacecraft to send images from Mercury since 1975

Catch me if you can! I'm the speed-demon space probe that gave chase to the fastest planet in the solar system. It only took me six and a half years to reach swift Mercury!

Speed and nearness to the Sun make Mercury difficult to access. You need to bustle to catch up with it, yet the extra "kick" given by the Sun's gravitational force makes it very difficult to avoid overshooting. My voyage took me across 4.9 billion mi. (7.9 billion km) of space. I looped past the Sun 15 times and used the gravity of Earth, Venus, and even Mercury to steer my path. It's been worth the trip—viewing the planet from Earth is tricky, and it has kept its secrets well hidden. I've returned fantastic images and even found water ice lurking in permanently shadowed areas— amazing for a planet that reaches 806°F (430°C) in the Sun!

● Launch date: August 3, 2004
● Number of images collected by *MESSENGER*: more than 100,000
● Name stands for **ME**rcury **S**urface, **S**pace **EN**vironment, **GE**ochemistry, and **R**anging

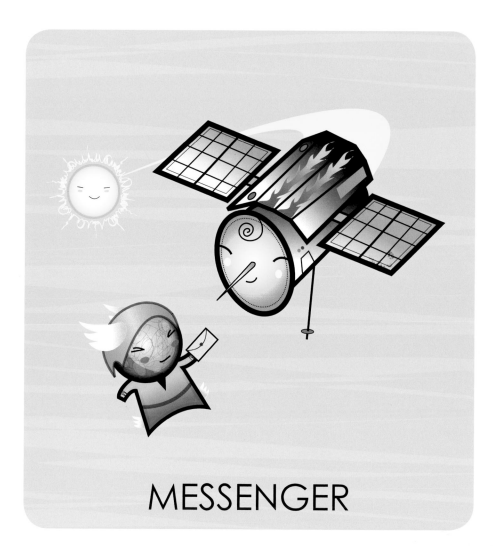

MESSENGER

Venus Express
■ Sunshine Superstars

✴ A European Space Agency (ESA) probe orbiting Venus
✴ Aims to understand how the planet's climate works
✴ Also plans to see if there is current volcanic activity on Venus

All aboard the express train to Venus! I am a souped-up refit of ESA's *Mars Express* spacecraft, toughened to withstand the extreme conditions of our planetary neighbor. I'm talking intense solar heating and a barrage of radiation!

Modest Venus hides her charms beneath a thick, toxic atmosphere. Choking clouds of sulfuric acid keep her surface invisible to telescopes on Earth. I'm studying her cloud systems and atmosphere. My cloud-penetrating radar is building a map of surface temperatures, while other instruments analyze the cloud layers. The almost pure carbon dioxide atmosphere bottles up the Sun's heat and keeps the planet's surface hot enough to melt lead. It's too late for Venus to reverse this "greenhouse effect," but if I can find the "point of no return," I might save Earth.

● Launch date: November 9, 2005
● Expected end of mission: December 2014
● Proportion of carbon dioxide in Venus's atmosphere: 96%

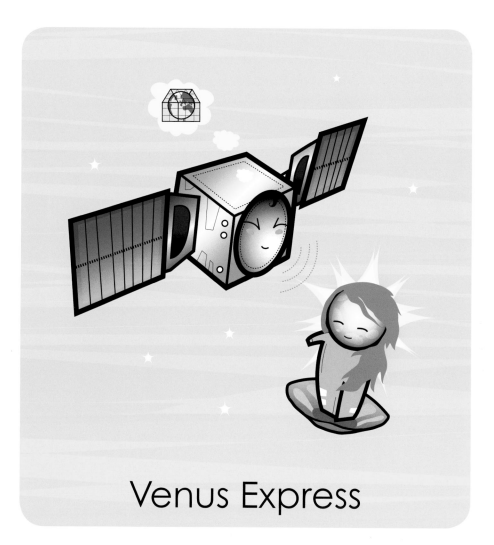

Venus Express

Sputnik 1
Sunshine Superstars

✷ Earth's very first artificial satellite
✷ Transmitted its bleep for 22 days until its batteries ran down
✷ Kick-started the Space Race between the Soviets and the U.S.A.

Back in the day, it was me who showed the world that human-made objects could be placed in orbit around Earth and above the atmosphere. No bigger than an exercise ball with four long, trailing antennae, I looked like a metal jellyfish. Once above Earth, I started to transmit my beep-beep message and my signal was picked up all around the world by radio hacks.

Sputnik 1

● Launch date: October 4, 1957
● Size of metal sphere: 23 in. (58.5cm) in diameter
● Number of Earth orbits: 1,440

Satellite

Sunshine Superstars

- ✴ A computer-controlled machine in orbit around Earth
- ✴ Equipped with power, recording instruments, and radio
- ✴ Occasionally seen at night—looks like a star on the move

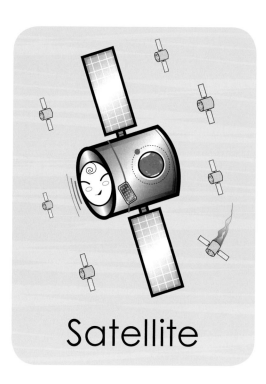

Satellite

I'm your tireless servant in the sky. Orbiting silently overhead, I monitor the planet's weather and carry telephone calls and TV signals. I operate the Global Positioning System (GPS), so you always know where you are. Sometimes I spy on people, too, so be good now! I mostly hang out in low Earth orbit (LEO), where life ends in a blaze of glory when I burn up in Earth's atmosphere.

- Weather satellite orbital period: 100 minutes (polar orbit)
- Low Earth orbit: 75 to 1,240 mi. (120 to 2,000km) above Earth's surface
- Number of satellites currently orbiting Earth: 1,000

Mars Reconnaissance Orbiter

Sunshine Superstars

* The largest of the space probes currently orbiting Mars
* Searches for signs of past water on this bone-dry planet
* Snapped *Curiosity* landing on Mars in 2012

I'm the big dog of the Mars expedition team. Built using ultramodern carbon-composite materials and carrying a titanium fuel tank, I'm a high-tech hound, too!

I'm one sharp-eyed observer. Equipped with the biggest high-resolution camera ever seen on a robot spacecraft, I map the planet and scour it for evidence of past lakes and seas, such as old shorelines. I also look for good landing sites for future Mars missions and picked out a spot for the *Phoenix* lander of 2008. One of my main duties is to provide a daily weather report from the red planet, but I also act as a relay station *par excellence*, feeding data from other spacecraft and rover robots on the surface back to Earth.

- Launch date: August 12, 2005
- Name of biggest camera: HiRISE (**Hi**gh **R**esolution **I**maging **S**cience **E**xperiment)
- Spacecraft and launch cost: $720 million

Mars Reconnaissance Orbiter

Curiosity
Sunshine Superstars

- ☀ NASA's Mars Science Laboratory (MSL) rover
- ☀ *Curiosity* is unmanned and controlled exclusively from Earth
- ☀ You can follow *Curiosity*'s progress on Twitter

Call me Rover! I am a car-size puppy, super keen and ready to explore—the ultimate remote-controlled robot. I'm sniffing around for the scent of life on the red planet.

I landed in Gale Crater in 2012 after the most amazing egg drop in history. Nicknamed the "Seven Minutes of Terror," it involved an unlikely combination of parachute, "sky-crane," and rockets, but I touched down safely. I am a laboratory on wheels, with 17 high-tech cameras, a laser that can vaporize a rock at seven paces, a rock drill, and scientific instruments to analyze the chemical content of the Martian soil. Mars today is a dry, dead world, but if life once existed on the planet, it might have left chemical traces of its passing in the rocks. So far, no luck, but I'll keep on looking "doggedly"!

- ● Launch date: November 26, 2011
- ● Communications delay between Earth and Mars: about 14 minutes
- ● Top speed of travel: 295 ft. (90m) per hour (regular speed 98 ft./30m per hour)

Curiosity

Dawn
Sunshine Superstars

✳ NASA spacecraft visiting the asteroids Vesta and Ceres
✳ Tasked with learning about the formation of the solar system
✳ The first NASA probe to orbit two separate bodies

Mine was an ugly duckling mission that was canceled, reinstated, then postponed before finally getting off the ground. Once I took wing, however, I soared magnificently and exceeded everybody's expectations.

I roam the asteroid belt between Mars and Jupiter, to visit two of its largest members—both "starter planets" that stopped growing at an early age. I aim to find out how planets formed in the young solar system, and why it is that some hold onto water while others lose it. To get around I use a propulsion engine called an ion drive. While Rocket works by throwing a lot of mass behind it to generate thrust, my ion drive throws out very small masses at eye-watering speeds to achieve the same effect. It means I don't need to carry large amounts of heavy fuel with me. Zoooooom!

● Launch date: September 27, 2007
● Key dates: Vesta orbit entry: July 16, 2011; Ceres arrival: February 2015
● Length: 7.74 ft. (2.36m) (solar arrays retracted); 64.6 ft. (19.7m) (solar arrays extended)

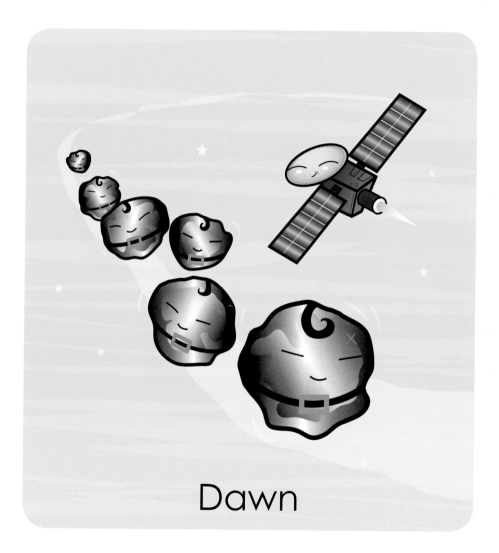

Dawn

Chapter 3
Outer Planetary Mob

Come and meet this hardened bunch of adventurers, the tough guys who mount expeditions to the outer planets, comets, and dwarf planets. Many of them belong to NASA's Flagship Program and count among the biggest and heaviest spacecraft ever launched. Short "launch windows" open when planets are reachable with a minimal outlay of energy. It means that space probes can minimize fuel and maximize onboard science equipment. Out in the wilds of the solar system, the cold and lack of sunlight make power a big issue. All of these explorers will perish out in space, and none will ever return to Earth . . .

Voyager 1 and 2

Galileo

Cassini-Huygens

New Horizons

Rosetta

Voyager 1 and 2
■ Outer Planetary Mob

※ These seasoned explorers embarked on a Grand Tour in 1977
※ V2 took in Jupiter, Saturn, Uranus, and Neptune
※ V1 discovered Jupiter's rings and volcanoes on its moon, Io

Veterans from another era, we are man's longest-serving spacecraft. We have looped through the solar system and are now about to enter interstellar space. Currently over 100 times more distant from Earth than the Sun is, we are officially the planet's most remote human-made objects.

We have visited the four biggest planets, sending home incredible snapshots. In 1990, *Voyager 1* looked back toward Earth and took a famous series of shots showing our planet as a "pale blue dot," half a pixel big. *Voyager 1*'s last action will be to study the "magnetic highway" at the very edge of the Sun's influence. Sadly, our electrical supply will begin to run low in about 2020, and although our controllers will shut down our systems one-by-one to prolong our lives, we oldies will finally blink out in 2025.

● Launch dates: August 20, 1977 (*V2*); September 5, 1977 (*V1*)
● Distance from Earth: 11.5 billion mi. (18.5 billion km) (*V1*, February 2013)
● Number of work years devoted to the Voyager project: 11,000

Voyager 1 and 2

Galileo
■ Outer Planetary Mob

☀ Space probe from NASA's Flagship Program that orbited Jupiter
☀ Named after the father of telescopic astronomy, Galileo Galilei
☀ Discovered clouds of ammonia in Jupiter's atmosphere

I am one big beast! Launched by the Space Shuttle *Atlantis*, I swung around Venus and Earth and looped toward my destination—the giant planet, Jupiter.

I saw close-ups of Jupiter's thin rings and found evidence that its icy moons might hold onto thin atmospheres. On July 13, 1995, I released an onboard probe—a kind of mini me—that parachuted into the cloud deck and took samples of Jupiter's dense atmosphere. Then, in 2003, I was driven into the planet! That's right, I was deliberately destroyed to avoid contaminating Jupiter's moons with any of Earth's bacteria that might have hitched a lift into space. Within no time, I was gone. Crushed, melted, and vaporized, I became part of Jupiter's atmosphere, leaving my spot open for *Juno*, set to arrive at Jupiter in 2016.

● Launch date: October 18, 1989
● Number of Jupiter orbits: 35
● Speed of travel at time of impact at end of mission: 30 mi. (48km) per second

Galileo

Cassini-Huygens
■ Outer Planetary Mob

☀ Spacecraft combo from NASA (*Cassini*) and ESA (*Huygens*)
☀ The first spacecraft to operate in orbit around Saturn
☀ *Cassini* discovered clouds swirling like water in a drain

We consist of *Huygens* attached to *Cassini*, piggyback fashion, and we've made history as one of the most complicated spacecraft ever built. Powered by *Cassini*'s red-hot pellets of radioactive plutonium, our joint mission is to study Saturn's rings, atmosphere, and moons.

Pint-size *Huygens* (say "hoy-gens") is a landing probe sent to explore Saturn's biggest moon, Titan. Meanwhile, big-boy *Cassini* is conducting more than 25 investigations of the ringed planet. On January 14, 2005, fearless *Huygens* plunged into Titan's atmosphere. It punched through the thick, swirling clouds—freefalling at speeds reaching 4 mi. (6km) per second and withstanding blistering temperatures of 32,000°F (18,000°C)—to give humans never-before-seen pictures of Titan's spooky methane lakes. That's some feat!

● Launch date: October 15, 1997
● Combined size: 22 ft. (6.7m) high; 13 ft. (4m) wide
● Time it takes for *Cassini*'s signals to reach Earth: 1.5 hours

Cassini-Huygens

New Horizons
■ Outer Planetary Mob

✴ The spacecraft on a white-knuckle ride to Pluto and beyond
✴ Made a successful Jupiter flyby in late 2006
✴ Now set to make a Pluto flyby in 2015

I'm a speed freak. Oh yeah, man! I set the record for the fastest launch from Earth, flung by an *Atlas V* rocket like a skipping stone across the blackness of space at 36,372 mi. (58,536km) per hour . . . a skipping stone the size of a grand piano!

I'm off to visit distant parts of the solar system—places not yet visited by spacecraft. When you travel this deep into space, far from the Sun, solar panels are of no use. I have an onboard nuclear power plant to keep me going! My target is the dwarf planet Pluto. My mission? To study it close up. I'll learn more about its geology and climate and might even spot ring systems or undiscovered moons. I'll pass within 6,200 mi. (10,000km) of Pluto and 16,800 mi. (27,000km) of its moon, Charon. But why stop there? I also have the unexplored, dark, and icy regions of the Kuiper Belt in my sights!

● Launch date: January 19, 2006
● Pluto encounter: July 14, 2015
● First images of Pluto released: November 28, 2006

New Horizons

Rosetta
■ Outer Planetary Mob

✳ Comet-chasing spacecraft from European Space Agency (ESA)
✳ *Rosetta* will make the first close-up investigation of a comet
✳ The lander *Philae* will use harpoons to touch down on the comet

I'm a comet chaser—an interstellar adventurer sent to unravel the mysteries of the solar system. I am set to discover how things were before the first planets formed. More than 4.6 billion years ago, the only things swirling around the Sun were comets and asteroids.

I plan to take a closer look at comet Churyumov-Gerasimenko. My twisted route involved four gravitational assists—maneuvers that use the gravity of a planet to fling a spaceship farther and faster on its way. So I whizzed past Earth and took a risky skim (the "Billion Euro Gamble") around the dark side of Mars, before voyaging onward to the main belt of asteroids. I'm equipped with a mini lander, *Philae*, which will attempt a touchdown on the comet in November 2014, to begin probing its icy surface. *Brr*!

● Launch date: March 2, 2004
● In deep-space hibernation (snooze mode): June 2011 to January 2014
● Span of *Rosetta*'s solar panel "wings": 105 ft. (32m) (tip to tip)

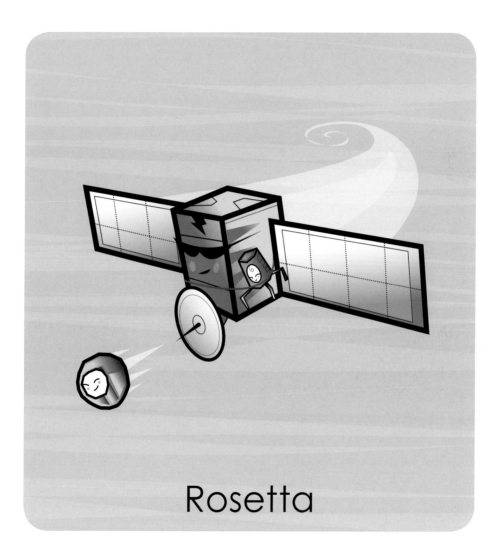

Rosetta

Chapter 4
Infinity and Beyond

With their sharp eyes firmly fixed on the glories of the universe and their dials set to "infinity and beyond," these go-getters seek the bigger picture. These critters are the über-geeks of space exploration—the ones who ask the most important questions about our 13.7-billion-year-old cosmos. Questions like: How did it all begin? (Planck); What does it look like? (Gaia); What is it made of? (Space Telescope); and is there anyone else out there . . . anyone at all? (Kepler and SETI). Hitch a ride with these high-tech dudes and it won't be long before you start hearing some answers. Prepare to be mind-boggled!

Space Telescope

Planck

Kepler

SETI

Gaia

Space Telescope

■ Infinity and Beyond

✷ Star of NASA's Great Observatories Program
✷ This eye-above-the-sky shows the universe in close-up
✷ The James Webb Space Telescope is set to launch in 2018

I'm a real paparazzo—I take photos of *actual* stars! Orbiting Earth, I have great views of objects in the solar system, but I spend most of my time peering into the Milky Way and beyond, into the great depths of space and time.

Of course there are powerful telescopes on Earth, too, but they mainly collect "visible light" images—ones that can be seen with the human eye. I, on the other hand, can tinker with X-ray and infrared images, which puts me in a different league altogether. I've shown observers what far-distant objects, such as galaxies, look like in close-up. Better still, I have revealed the very first galaxies created at the beginning of time. I've also shed light on the existence of extrasolar planets and might have found the youngest star ever seen. Far out!

● Hubble Space Telescope (HST): provides "visible light" images of the universe
● Spitzer Space Telescope (SST): provides "infrared light" images of the universe
● Chandra X-ray Observatory (CXO): provides X-ray images of the universe

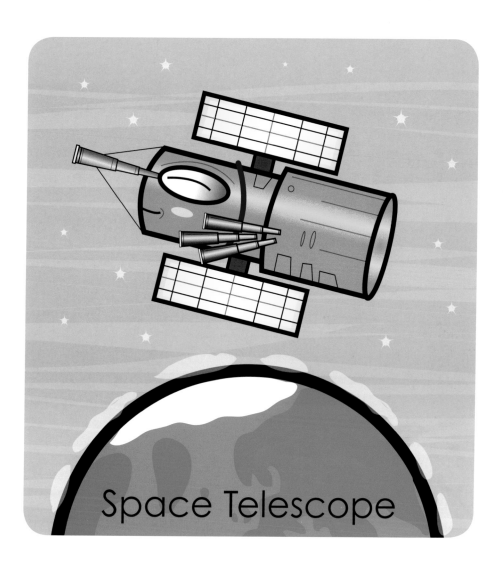

Space Telescope

Planck
■ Infinity and Beyond

☀ An ESA mission sent to study the energy left by the big bang
☀ It is checking the universe for signs of sudden "growth spurts"
☀ Gives a supersharp, all-sky survey at microwave wavelengths

First things first: I'm no plank! My funny name comes from famous German physicist Max Planck. I'm an ambitious little 'scope with the entire universe in my sights.

I want to find out what the universe was like way back when and the rate at which it's expanding. I'm measuring the soft glow of heat still remaining from the superhot explosion that kick-started the universe. These embers of the big bang are called the Cosmic Microwave Background (CMB). It's all around us, in every direction. The mystery I want to solve is how such a big, messy blast resulted in the "lumpy" universe we live in. You might expect an explosion to spread energy—and mass—evenly across space, but barely noticeable ripples gave rise to the galaxies of today's universe. I want to know why!

● Launch date: May 14, 2009
● Distance from Earth: 932,000 mi. (1.5 million km)
● Average temperature of CMB: −454°F (−270°C)

Planck

Kepler
■ Infinity and Beyond

✳ This space telescope trails Earth as it orbits the Sun
✳ Measures dips in the brightness of stars to locate alien worlds
✳ Named after Polish mathematician Johannes Kepler

I'm searching the night sky for Earth-like planets orbiting stars in the spiral arms of the Milky Way Galaxy. My mission is to locate similar-size planets in the habitable zone, where liquid water might be found on the surface of rocky worlds.

Unlike Space Telescope, which focuses in on individual objects in the sky, I scan a huge star field. I point north toward the constellations of Cygnus and Lyra. That way, no stray light from the Sun can creep in on my instruments. Fixing a star in my sights for hundreds of hours, I look for telltale "winks"—barely noticeable dips in the brightness of a star when a planet passes in front of it. I have been hugely successful and have spotted the smallest planet ever detected, the first six-planet system, and double-star planets. Could these places be home to alien life?

● Launch date: March 6, 2009
● Number of stars in Kepler's field of view: more than 100,000
● Orbital period: 372.5 Earth days

Kepler

SETI
■ Infinity and Beyond

✳ A needle-in-a-haystack **S**earch for **E**xtra**T**errestrial **I**ntelligence!
✳ Attempts to find out whether we are truly alone in the universe
✳ Messages to potential aliens have never been returned

Is anybody out there? Life has risen on Earth, so surely it must exist on another of the galaxy's planets, right? Or are such circumstances very special and unlikely? Perhaps it's only *intelligent* life that is extremely rare, or maybe other civilizations are not interested in making contact. Well, I've been straining my eyes and ears for decades, and the only signal coming back from outer space is static.

SETI

● Messages to aliens: 1972/1973 (*Pioneer* plaques); 1977 (*Voyager* Golden Records)
● Possible alien communication: 1977 (Wow! signal; Perkins Observatory, U.S.A.)
● Most powerful message sent into space: Arecibo Message (1974)

Gaia
Infinity and Beyond

✷ ESA mission to make a three-dimensional map of the Milky Way
✷ Measures star distances and spots new asteroids
✷ Also doing some checks on Einstein's Theory of Relativity

Gaia

I am the mapmaker. Zipping through space, I've sure got my work cut out. I have to plot the positions of a billion stars in our galaxy. That's less than one percent of the Milky Way! I'll check each measurement 70 times to make the most accurate three-dimensional map ever made. My map will help figure out the dance of the stars and the forces exerted on the galaxy.

● Launch date: October 2013
● Orbital period: approximately 180 days
● Distance from Earth: 932,000 mi. (1.5 million km)

Index

N
Neptune 40
New Horizons **46**

O
Orbit **10**, 14, 16, 18, 20, 22, 24, 26, 28, 30, 31, 32, 36, 42, 44, 52, 56, 59, 62, 63

P
Planck 50, **54**
Pluto 46
polar orbit 10, 31
probes 10, 22, 26, 28, 32, 36, 38, 42, 44, 46, 62

R
radiation 12, 20, 22, 28, 63
Rocket **8**, 16, 34, 36
Rosetta **48**

S
Satellite 10, 16, 24, 30, **31**
Saturn 40, 44
Saturn V rocket 8, 14
SETI 50, **58**

solar system 4, 26, 36, 38, 40, 46, 48, 52, 62, 63, 64
space laboratory 16, 18, 34,
space missions 14, 15, 20, 22, 28, 32, 36, 44, 46, 54, 56, 59
Space Race 30, 64
Space Shuttle **16**, 42
space planes 16
Space Suit **12**
Space Telescope 16, 50, **52**, 56
Space Tourist **20**
Sputnik 1 10, **30**
Sputnik 2 4
STEREO **24**
Sun 10, 18, 20, 24, 26, 28, 38, 40, 46, 48, 56, 62, 64

U
Uranus 40

V
Venus 22, 26, 28, 42
Venus Express **28**
visible light 52, 63
Voyager 1 and 2 **40**

Glossary

Ammonia A naturally occurring chemical that is an important source of nitrogen for living things.

Asteroid A small rock in orbit around the Sun between the orbits of Mars and Jupiter.

big bang theory The idea that the universe was created in an enormous, hot fireball about 13.7 billion years ago.

Comet A dirty snowball looping the Sun with a long, elliptical (oval) orbit. Comets have one or two tails and, unlike planets, can appear in any part of the sky.

Constellation An area of the sky containing a pattern made by stars, as seen from Earth. Stars in the same constellation are at different distances from Earth.

Deep-space hibernation A kind of "snooze mode" for robotic spacecraft while they whiz across space toward their distant destinations.

Extrasolar planet A planet orbiting a different star than the Sun; belongs to an entirely different planetary system.

Galaxy A system of billions of stars, dust, and gas clouds (and sometimes black holes) held together by gravitational attraction.

Gravity The invisible force of attraction felt between objects that have mass. Gravity keeps the planets orbiting the Sun and the Moon orbiting Earth.

Interstellar space The regions of space in between the stars and beyond the influence of a star's "weather."

Invisible universe Objects in space that "shine" in those parts of the electromagnetic spectrum that are above and below the frequency of visible light. X-ray and ultraviolet are above; infrared and radio are below. They are both, therefore, invisible to the human eye.

Launch window The period of time when Earth's spin and its position on its orbit enable a spacecraft to be launched on its journey.

Mass A measure of the amount of matter in an object. Things with mass feel weight when attracted to another object by the force of gravity.

Methane A gas produced on Earth by living things (mainly by microbes, but also from farts). Some planets are also partly composed of methane.

Microwave Short-wavelength, high-frequency radio waves are known as microwaves.

Milky Way Our home galaxy—a barred spiral galaxy. Our solar system is located on the inner rim of one of its arms.

Orbital period The time taken for an object to make one complete revolution (orbit) around another body.

Payload Equipment carried by a rocket or launch vehicle. Payloads are stored in the payload bay.

Radiation Energy emitted by a body in the form of electromagnetic radiation (e.g. light) or fast-moving particles smaller than an atom.

Glossary

Solar array A sheet of solar panels used to convert sunlight into electricity.

Solar system The family of planets, moons, asteroids, meteoroids, comets, dust, and debris that orbits the Sun.

Space Race A competition between nations to be the first to do something in space. The United States and U.S.S.R. raced against each other to put a man on the Moon in the 1950s and 1960s.

Static A crackling hiss that can be picked up by radios, TVs, phones, satellites, and radio telescopes. Most of it is generated by natural electricity on Earth—e.g. lightning— but a small portion comes from the big bang explosion.

Terrestrial planet A rocky planet, such as the four inner planets of the solar system.

Theory of Relativity Albert Einstein's theory that mass can be converted into energy and that the speed of light in a vacuum is always the same.

Vacuum A region of space that contains almost no matter.

Velocity The speed of an object traveling in a particular direction.

Visible light The part of the electromagnetic spectrum to which a human's eyes are sensitive.